The Nectar-Nook

The Nectar-Nook

Tuhin Sanyal

Chitrangi

Published by: *Chitrangi*, A-10/1, Amarabati, Sodepur, Calcutta 700110.

First edition: September, 2016

Printed at: S. P. Communications

Contact
Email: thethirdeyeimprint@gmail.com

Cover illustration & design: Chitrangi

ISBN-13: 97893-85783-81-4

Price: INR 200

FOREWORD

A FOREWORD to this tavern is "wholesome thirst,
insane!"
Every peg-measure is a 'Rubaii', quatrain,
Or, say, eight half-lines, if you be measurer keen,
'A ton, three tens and five' verses have herein
Been slowly churned for 'RAINA'— my only little girl—
The honing of whose brew in a January did unfurl!
My Nectar made her Soul, her content and her form
Were crafted in my senses, in winsome poetic norm!

CONTENTS

CONTENTS cannot be differentiated, nor by Me nor You!
The Po(r)tions of this Poem have cadences Pure and True,
Well mixed up; churned and poured, for the Finesse of the Brew!

Yet, in Tipsy sequence— Winter, Summer, Fall—
The Malts of Souls reveal themselves herein. In all,
O Mind, Body, Universe, pay heed as Nectars call!

Now Taste it, Sip and Gurgle, Roll it in Human Head—
This Golden Brew in Cup Archaic, Saki in Modern tread,
Timeless— this Silky Rheum; Free-flowing, Wine-Red!

1
Of Grapes galore, of Feelings soft,
Well-wrought, I bring this Liquid form,
Darling, hold my Cup aloft,[1]
And take a Sip in simple norm;
First, to You, my Offering goes,
With remnants all the World I'll treat;
Foremost 'Welcome' for you, Love—
My Nectar-Nook— here you Surfeit!

2
If you do Thirst, then I shall Heat
The Universe for all its Ale,
Your Saki,[2] I, on a single foot,
Shall cup a dance[3] in Stupor-Dale;
Nectars of this life have struck
You with sweetness much, so true!
This day I may empty upon you
Liquid Vines[4] which heavens brew.

3
Darling, you are my wine-urn,
And thus, I am your thirsty cup,
Pour yourself in me and turn
A regular visitor of the pub;
O'erbrimming, I fill to spill you,
On drinking me you've tipsy been,
We, some twosome, awesome form
The True-Together-Hippocrene.[5]

4
Philosophies from vines drew
Liquors of preponderance,
Poet and Saki in me fuse,[6]
Cupping poesy's sacraments;[7]
Not a corner will be slack,
Lucky lakhs, drink by the lee![8]
Readers True are Drinkers' pack;[9]
My Verse— A 'Pub', for the dreary.[10]

5

With musings[11] sweet of sweeter thoughts
I daily, gaily make the drink,
At will I fill my Soulful Cup
With sweetness to its thirsty brink;
Hands phantasmal[12] cup uphold,
In soulful spree I drink the ale;
Myself be Barmaid, Barman,
Drinker and the Wine-Dale!

6

Pub-ward bound from his home,
Heads the Drinker for his Urn,
"Which road to take?" in naivetté[13] asks—
His dilemma[14] so taciturn;[15]
Varied paths do people show,
As for me, I must tell you—
'Tread[16] upon your Path and know
You shall find the Tavern True.'

7

I walked my life, in walking spent
The greater part of life, alack![17]
"'Tis farther still", in parrot-strut
Says every soul who shows the track;
I lack boldness to forward move,
Lack courage to course[18] retrace;
At a loss! — transfixes[19] me,
Yonder[20] Tavern's distant face.

8

Constantly strut[21]— "Wine-Dale,
Intoxicating Liqueur[22] hale,"
Fancy with your feeling hands
Cup-claret-fantastic-ale;[23]
Concentrate in honeyed soul
On handsome barmen, barmaids whole,
And farther walk, O Journeyman
To close up to your Drinking Bowl.[24]

9

To drink at will to the drinker's fill
If itself turns intoxicant,[25]
Desperate, the lips reflect
Wine pegs in wishful chant,
If Bartender then concentrates,
Succeeds in slimy Alcohol,
Friend! No Saki, Peg, nor Ale,
You shall reach your Drinking Hall.

10

Hark![26] Lapping trills the falling dew
From honey-pots to pegs anew,
Hark!   Slopping, slipping, distributing—
The Barmaid—! All her ale, to you;
Here we reach, and not too far,
Just ought to walk you four steps hence;
Serene… hark! The drunkards' din![27]
Smell the Tavern's Ale-incense.

11

Water-soiree's[28] strumming[29] ale
Binds cup to cup in lip-lock[30] tale,
Lyres lure-in limerick[31] pure
With limbeck-bearer's[32] swaying grail,
The moulding[33] liquor's scolding flail[34]
In a drumming seller's noisy ale
Enhances the tipsiness,
The drunken din of Nectar-Dale.

12

Henna-ornate[35] silky palm,
Gem-beaded-cup-nectar-ale,[36]
Muffling crepes,[37] like wine-grapes
On the Golden Geisha[38] of the Grail;[39]
Head— Purple-geared, and bust in Teal,[40]
A-drinking did their spirits peal;[41]
A tryst[42] it set, Nook took the bet,
To race its wine with rainbow-zeal.[43]

13

Before the cup is in your clutch,
She will flaunt her indignance,[44]
Before you press your lips on hers
She'll humour[45] you in temperance,[46]
Before the barmaids, barmen come,
Many refusals shall you face;
Be undaunted[47], Journeyman,
Wine's frisky[48] in the first place.

14

"Red-riding-rheum, sharp and wrought,[49]
A volcano in sense begot"—[50]
Dub not so that surfing[51] ale,
Nor— "rheum[52] where bosom's blisters blot,"
This sifted[53] ale loves gifted pain,
Old Memories— Saki— stain,
Pang's[54] pliant[55] cask![56] there if you bask,
Reach my Pang-Pub time-n-again.[57]

15

The liquid half of earth is cold,
Traveller, such is not my Ale!
Mundane[58] cups cold liquid hold,
My vial's[59] warmth can never fail;
Volcanic ale…that burning grail
Are poesies[60] of a smitten[61] heart;
Though fires affright[62], I welcome those
With boldness, to my Liqueur-Mart.

16

The flowing ale in a stormy cup
Is sighted, lifted to the lip,
Lo! The cup will touch, impinge[63]
And singe[64] your lips with every sip;
"If bodies burn when lips are done,
I still would thirst for droplets two"—
Hark!   Musing, Boozing[65] Bedlam[66] Lot,
Your Liquor-Dale is calling you.

17
When Holy-Books have burnt someone's
Volcanic fires of the Soul,
With Temples, Mosques and Churches broken,
Tipsy One hath taken toll,
From Pundits', Momins', Clergies'[67] mesh[68]
That Tipsy One on teething through,[69]
Is welcome to my soulful ale—
A House too full with Bedlam-Brew.

18
Salivating lips to lack,
Liquid jouissance[70] not to kiss,
In throbbing clutches not to hold
A wine-peg — Ah, mammoth[71] miss!
If ye[72] with barmen, barmaids coy,
In tipsy bouts[73] have flirted not,
Blasphemy![74] 'Tis a wry and dry[75]
Life's Ale-Dale for such a lot.[76]

19

Worshipper turns 'Wine Server',
'Lover'! His sacred Ganges[77] is
The selfsame[78] ale, when pegs are beads
For telling at the Rosaries,[79]
"Come drink some more, here's wine galore"— [80]
May this chant[81] be a Prayer new,
Be idol, I, o' the Doping Lord,[82]
Turn this Pub to a Temple True.

20

No bell did toll[83] in temple, true,
No garland did the idol see,
The muezzin[84] of the mosque sat home
And placed it under lock and key,
Treasures of the kings did go,
Looted, fell the fortress-walls;
All hail[85] be the drinking folks!
Stay ajar[86] these Drinking Halls.

21

Dynasties have fallen thus,
On their graves not one to cry,
Palaces turn loners,[87] where
Now trilling,[88] lilting[89] dancers vie;
Regal estates tumble down,
Their Lady Luck[90] to snoring takes,
But Drinkers will their Goblets hold
As wide awake the Tavern rakes.[91]

22

Aye,[92] all will end, yet they will not—
The Sweet Ale-Bearers, Black as Death,[93]
Juices all will dwindle,[94] but
Winsome[95] Ale shall flow, in faith;[96]
Dud[97] and desolate[98] they will turn—
The Swarming, jovial, jamborees,[99]
Urns of Death shall sentinel[100]
With Sleepless Tavern's wakeful ease.

23

A worldly pass on wine dubs
The peg 'bedlam' and 'frisky' ale,
'Picturesque She'[101]— limbeck bearer,
'Peerless'[102]— the drunkard hale,
How shall they fare?[103] Lopsided[104] pair—
The public-house and world— a-brace![105]
When daily earth is a doleful[106] share,[107]
The Wine-Dale has a bridal face.

24

Psychotics— who teetotal— [108]
Teething,[109] term this tavern 'vile',[110]
On boozing[111] doth their railing[112] fall,
Their jaws are lock'd with ale, beguile![113]
Slave and rebel equal feel
The winsome ale, the tipsy cup;
Fine, with world-wide-winsome-wine
This Victory-Tavern I hold up.

25

E'ergreen tavern's fullness fair
O'erlooks that world at large,
(There) Morbid[114] Muharram[115] looms[116], and here
'Tis happy[117] Holika's[118] fiery surge;[119]
Directly from the heavens hailed[120]
To this earth— no sorrow knows,
Glum[121] world besides, Glam[122] Tavern basks
In a festive Eid[123] of jocund[124] shows.[125]

26

Once a year the fire looms—[126]
Festive Holi's[127] fiery heave,[128]
Only once are bets a-flung—[129]
Garlands of a lamp-lit eve!
O worldly lot, do come some day,
You'll find this pub in sparkle-hue,
(Here) Days are Holi! Nights, Diwali!—[130]
Festive-Nook shall engulf you!

27

Who doth not know, a Human born,
Is Born to Drink? Who doth not know
That Rearer,[131] Bearer,[132] Suckling Server's[133]
Nurture-Ale,[134] that Milky store?
A Birth's benison—[135] Life's potion[136]
Humans drink; for this reason
Foremost, Man is Born to Drink—
Mother's Milk! First Ale-Season!

28

May the vineyard tendrils hold
Their ground to give us wine hale,
Eternal be that sod[137] which God
Has formed to chalice Nectar Ale,
May the vinous,[138] guzzling[139] thirst
Insatiate,[140] disquiet stay,
Eternal be the drinking lot,
Their Tavern and their Ale foray.[141]

29

I'm fine, in troth![142] I wish they too
Stay fine— those barmen, barmaids all,
Since tipsy-toes[143] are indifferent
To omens,[144] or what may befall,[145]
Pray,[146] ask me not if I am fine,
Ask that of the House of Ale,
In chorus hail no Lord you trust,
In chorus chant— "Hail Liquor-Dale!"

30

'Trader' Sol[147] sells Nectar hale,[148]
Jug— 'Indus Creek',[149] Ale— 'Wine' becomes,
Clouds recur[150] as 'Limbeck-Bearers,'
Earth— the 'Cup'— holds vinous charms;
Impinging,[151] reeling,[152] Raining Wine
Drenches,[153] quenches![154] Tulips, Ferns,
Jasmines, Thirsting Grass I be;
The Tavern takes new Monsoon turns.

31

Gem-stuck, star-spangled[155] Sky—
A cup holding all vinous charms—
If inverted, and Ocean-blue
Is inserted, it wine becomes!
Tempest, Gale,[156] ale-servers be,
Spill 'pon lips, in wine immerse,[158]
Stretching on the ocean strands;
The Tavern becomes the Universe.

32

On lips though juices sundry[159] ply,[160]
The tongue will feel the wine taste,
An oddment,[161] oft, the palms may hold
Yet take it for a Glass at best;
Faces to faces Transform,
Seem wine-bearers' faces… All;
Whatever may come in ken,[162]
The eyes behold the Drinking Hall.

33

The plants entwine in serving wine
In blossoms, take those flowering urns
Which haply[163] fill in sweeten'd will[164]
All that fragrant nectar churns;[165]
Mendicant…[166] the apian[167] chant—
Sips nectar, the swarm[168] of bees—
Their leaps and bounds in wine abound;
Meadows,[169] ope'[170] thy Tavern Trees!

34

Drip juicy trees like Saki-girls,
All blossoms then chalice be;
Nature's whim, they overbrim,[171]
Ah! Maddening perfumery![172]
On tasting[173] it the cuckoo birds
Tipsy turn, on branches coo,[174]
In Honey-Spring of fruition[175] seasons
Stays awake the Tavern True.

35

Make goblets[176] of the lulling[177] gale,
Honey'd season's fragrant[178] ale
Fills, refills, the breeze instills,[179]
Drunken stupor's[180] tipsy tale;
Nascent[181] green, the branching sheen[182]
Of peaceful bowers,[183] blissful[184] look,
In towing,[185] bowing, dancing turns
The Forest to a Nectar-Nook.

36

Make a Serving Sheila[186] of the Dawn,
Comes Twilight, then sunlit Morn;
A Starry soiree's token tweed[187]
The Earth pays up to Ale adorn,[188]
The birds too drink from myriad[189] rays,
To lose themselves[190] to tipsy trills;
Every Morn, from Nature born—
A Tavern 'tis,[191] of Sunlit thrills!

37

Out!   Morning rout[192] of a drunken bout,
Here's a Sheila of the Dusk,
Past ageing, assuaging[193]
The waning[194] wine, the constant cask!
Willy-nilly…[195] anomaly,[196]
Grief, this potion terminates,
When ale-guzzlers are slumber-struck,[197]
The Tavern stays awake, and waits.

38

Ale-trader is Darkness all,
Bounty-Barmaid[198]— Lunar Doll,
In every beam doth overbrim
Her waxing[199] wine's winsome thrall;[200]
Her lunar dose[201] makes drunkards lose
Their consciousness, in dozing ways
They Twinkle with the blinking Stars,
No Night becomes the Tavern's face.

39

As Visions shove, my Eyes rove[202]
But come to rest on Ale at last,
From fickle[203] ken my eyes again
Turn to view the peg steadfast,[204]
Whichever way may vision stray,[205]
I see Saki, barmaids all,
Whate'er fold my eyes behold
They end up at the Drinking Hall.

40

Barmaid Fair transforms to Flute
And flaunts[206] the chalice on her palm,
In which Juices (slopping[207] flow
Of liquid lips) do ale embalm;[208]
On courting[209] her the Yogi King[210]
Is named the 'Darling Dancer!' Look,
Be all equal, sorts big or small
Dance to the lilt of Nectar-Nook.

41

Ale-seller turns Piper then,
Serves the notes[211] of nectar lilt,
Sonatina-Saki[212] serves
A lyric-chalice to the hilt,[213]
On signals from the Piper's end
She runs through minors, majors, sharp,[214]
Treats the listeners to a toast[215]
That resonates[216] the Tavern Harp.

42

With winsome paint the Saki comes
As Painter, with the Brush-Vial,
From which to make us drink the spree[217]
Of Rainbows on a Sun-dial,[218]
Sip-by-sip it paints the soul's
Pictures all… in Hues[219] and Shades,
The Canvas holds the dancing form
Of a Nectar-Nook that captivates.

43

Intense green… vines wean—[220]
Steering act of shearing[221] ale,
Lotus-sun-soft-sapling-buds
Flower,[222] form the chalice hale;
Floral tremors— claret Sakis—
Filled with jewel'd Nectar Grace,
The drinking drake[223] in stupor hones[224]
A Mind-Wrought Lake—[225] the Tavern face.

44

The Snowy Peaks as Vines spread,
Icy Waters turn to ale,
Roving Rivers barmaids be
And fill the cups of Furrow Dale,
Meanderings and Soft Gurgling
Night and Day spill Motion Brook,
Fluttering Farmlands feed on 'em[226]
And India is a Nectar-Nook.

45

Great Sons of the Nation bleed
From their Hearts, forms Ruddy Ale,—
Bold Heads of her Daring Sons
The Saki Nation holds as Grail;
Charity, Compassion fuse,
India— 'The Mother' becomes;
A Blood-Thirsty Goddess[227]— 'Freedom!'
Pub turns 'Altar,'[228] Death benumbs.

46

Hurl slang galore, the mosque, encore[229]
Dubbed me drunkard, turn'd me out,
From temple door, they cursed me more,
For they saw me holding goblet stout;
Where in the world would my address—
For an atheist[230] so luckless—
Be? Were not my haven[231] true
The Refuge-Tavern's kind ingress.[232]

47

Turning tramp,[233] I wander thus,
I find wine in every place,
Whichever way my gait[234] may stray
I find the Saki, Goblet-grace.
For halting, Friends, no pang I feel,
None can keep me faith-bereft,[235]
Though Mosque or Temple found I none,
I found my Pub, to which I cleft.[236]

48

"No praying lot,[237] nor mosque be deck'd"—[238]
Says Allah in His words divine,
The barmaid but dolls up[239] to serve
Dandy[240] drinkers winsome wine,
Compare not your mosque, O Sheikh,[241]
With this minion[242] Madeira Mart,
Your mosque— an ageless widow, Sheikh;
Eternal bride— this Nectar-Hut!

49

With playing tunes, the praying lot
Forgot Allah's[243] holiness,
Though thunder struck, Attention-Ale…
Engrossed drunkards in its lays,
No offence I mean, O Sheikh!
Precisely, your mosque will learn
Attentiveness for ages hence,
As taught (since yore)[244] by True Tavern.

50

'Hindu, Muslim'— sects are two,
They drink but from the goblet same,
They share the single Nectar-Nook,
The tavern-wine, the guzzling game;
That Hindu-Muslim sync[245] would come
If mosques-n-temples were built straight,
Mosques and temples heighten feud,[246]
In Nectar-Nook they amalgamate.[247]

51

Sheikh, Namaazi,[248] beaded Pundit—[249]
Whoe'er— of the praying throng,
Howsoever he might hate
Ale, madeira,[250] all along,
Let him pass the tavern once
And I'd bet, with all my breath,
One wouldn't see him fain[251] refrain[252]
From Beckoning[253] Tavern's reckoning;[254] faith![255]

52

And the nectars tasty seem
Till wines with due distance club,[256]
All chalices haughty[257] feel
Till ushering in of th'[258] drinking cup,
Offer prayers, Pundit, Sheikh,
In thy mosque and temple till
The wine cask does well unmask,
Or the Nectar-Nook unveils[259] at will.

53

A taboo[260] today the world may hold,
The morrow[261] shall but see it drink,
This day it may shy away but
Tomorrow shall grant goblet-kink;[262]
Give a Wine-Prophet[263]— Ale Mahomet—[264]
To this world and you shall see,
Where now stands a temple, mosque,
Public houses there shall be.

54

Shimmering,[265] holy-fires like
Furnaces do ale distill;[266]
As holy sages meditate,
So spongy[267] selves are sitting still;
As daughters of the sages bear
Pitchers, so do Saki girls,
No less than some prayer place
My Prayer-Pious Pub unfurls.

55

Our ancestors would 'Soma'[268] drink,
In trendy tweet[269] we term it Ale;
Well-Wrought Urn, jug'd Nectar Wine
Of Drona,[270] is now Tumbler Hale;
Since drinking is a Vedic ritual,
O Traders of the Vedic thought,
Shun[271] it not; since ages old
We worship Taverns, nectar-wrought.

56

In Myth they churned the sea 'Varuni'[272]
And extracted the ale sublime,[273]
Ace enchantress Rambha's[274] daughters
Are 'barmaids' termed, in earthly time;
What Gods and Demons together brought,
Will saints and godmen wipe, censure?
One's mettle,[275] to ale withstand,[276]
Is understood by Tavern Pure.

57

Never can one hear, "That man
Has touched, defiled[277] my wine, alas!"
None complains, "That lowly man
Was drinking from my wine glass;"
People from all walks of life,
All sects, here do booze and buzz,[278]
The noble job of a ton[279] reformers
Noble Tavern singly[280] does.

58

Toils,[281] troubles, sorrows all, you
Forget with your drinking dole,[282]
You'd learn a lesson great if you
Stay Surfeited in your Soul;
As Lord's Folk you fall futile,[283]
You're better off as Wine's Men;
Lord-keepers may turn you out,
But Pub beckons with welcome-ken.[284]

59

In a way She welcomes all—
The wine-serving enchantress,
Naïve[285] men and learned souls
Are no different in drunkenness;
Kings and paupers equal are
In this preaching Nectar-Nook,
Of 'Equality'[286] it preaches first
In its pub-born[287] theory book.

60

This day I may have not reached
Forward for a cup again,
For peg o'er peg I did not beg
Yet dub me not a drunkard 'plain,'[288]
Wares galore you have in store,
Let shyness shun me, I shall take
More; and from my vocal thrill,
The Nectar-Nook with echoes rake.

61
Tomorrow? — No 'morrow' is
Awaited by a Drinker True,
Unhand[289] not the peg today,
Tomorrow may be numbing you;
What's in hand today may go,
Who can trust that morrow's flail?
'Tomorrow' does not shape my pub,
'Crafty Time' dubs Wine Dale.

62
My chance today is gifted; why
Mustn't I taste nectar-strewn
Rheum, and why not gaily fill
My peg, in moments opportune?
Why mustn't I with barmaids shy
Flirt today to heart's content?
This Liqueur-Dale of life, to us
Is Granted once, as Graces[290] lent.

63
Enliven[291] it today Darling,
Shimmering cup of bickering[292] lips,
Fill, fill, fill that luscious[293] cup
With youthfulness, whence nectar drips,[294]
Once you lock your lips with mine,
Pray, forget unlocking the pair,
Weariless, I'll drink you whole,
In Love-Dale of this Liqueur Fair.

64
Pretty lass, your countenance[295]
Itself is my goblet gold,
In which lap gem-nectar, sap
Of winsome ale in tipsy fold;
Doubling up, for dual[296] roles—
The drunkard and the barmaid—I—
Shall meet you surely at some place
To form the Tavern-tapestry.[297]

65

A two-day feat[298]—her nectar treat,
The barmaid gave me and got bored,
Dispassionate[299]—she fills my peg
Now, loveless passes it, once poured;
With attitudes of graces coy[300]
Or seeming love she serves me not,
Now-a-days her chalice serves
Wine which is duty-wrought.

66

This li'l measure[301] of life to love
And drink! But how much? Who can tell?
As I 'came' unto this earth
The "goer's" badge on me befell;
"Welcome," "adieu,"[302] all at once
Were readied simultaneously,
Uncork'd I my "Life, Death-nigh"[303]
And freely flowed in wine's spree.

67

What's to drink— till ceaselessly,[304]
Unflinchingly,[305] pour peg o'er peg?
What's to live for till assured
Of tavern-belle,[306] companion, keg?
Forfeiting-fears[307] are always near,
A-grind behind begetting-glee,
Gaiety[308] plies yet glee denies
That Ale-begetting Tapestry!

68

Scant[309] it is, my thirst to quench,
Meagre ale that you have brought!
Flaunt the clumsy cup you clutch,
Yet know, the thing is not well wrought!
'Tis good to die with Ocean's Thirst
Than drink this meagre, paltry share,
An "Indus-Thirst" is crafted by
That droplet-like Tavern's snare! [310]

69

What say you? 'Tis no more held
Dear by you— that flowing ale?
What say you? Those useless wreaths
Of tipsy-turvy pegs here fail?
Thirst you, stout, in a guzzling bout?
Endless then your Thirst shall be,
The tavern calls to quench your thirst
Yet whets[311] your thirst, Eternally.

70

"Lady Luck shall 'lot to thee,
And lotted[312] wine thou shalt get,"
Fate happens to forebode all,
And to his tune your cup is set,
Throw tantrums[313] O drinking lot,
It won't change your luck, alack!
All beget their lotted shares
Of tavern, wine and peg, arrack.[314]

71

Well, go ahead, act miserly
In giving me the promised drink,
Yes, go ahead and give me this
Broken peg with a ragged kink,
Patiently I dote[315] on these
But you shall rue them after me,
I won't come, my Memories
Shall haunt this pub, when I won't be.

72

Reverence, conceited[316] cares,
Or insults, after booze, lay by;
Shun'd pride, e'er since humble hands
Held the earthen goblet nigh;
In slighting coyness, Serving Lass,
Now I see no insult borne,
I got the boot[317] from all in sooth[318]
To find this tavern's Tipsy Zone.

73

Brittle,[319] temporal,[320] minute,[321] weak
Is the cup of human clay,
Within it, that bitter-sweet
Life's elixir[322] subtly lay,
'Death' becomes the cruel Saki
Spreading hundreds of her palms,
'Time' becomes the terrible guzzler,
'Eternity'— the tavern charms.

74

Someone formed me like a cup,
Filled elixir— brim to dregs,[323]
Wearied of the tipsy bout
I poured myself in wine pegs;
When the pangs of life arose,
I subdued them in goblets fine,
E'en before the birth of earth,
We Sakis, braved the tavern wine.

75

My luscious grape-like body bears
Wine, which I have thus instilled,
What say you, Sheikh, in hell will they
Roast me in the fiery field?
My Wine then shall stretch and draw,
And someone then shall drink from me,
While burning in hell-fires too
My Nectar-Nook I'll get to see.

76

When, Pluto-like, the God of Death
Comes, I'll drink and walk with him,
To Hell he'll take, yet hellish pains
I shall not feel with senses dim;
When unjust, cruel, crafty, curt
Gods of Death will thrash by flails,
Or lambaste[324] me with rods, my booze
Shall ensure that no pain entails.[325]

77
Wine-deep, if struts the lip
Of coupling, loving word or two,
Hearts of empty hands for once
If humoured were, by goblet-brew,
What loss, O World, would you incur? [326]
Malign[327] not my name in vain;
The solace[328] of a broken heart
Is— "toying with the Liquor-Den."

78
A sordid life in forgottance[329]
I pass, by guzzling Wine True,
The worries of a Sorry World
I shear, by lifting goblets few;
For willfulness, for taste or woe,
Drinks the world this hippocrene,
But I am of that ailing[330] lot
For whom this Ale is Medicine.

79

Drop by drop it daily drips,
Ah Darling, life's wine doth wane!
Wreckage acts in regular pacts
With th' crumbling cup— my body-bane;[331]
Enchantress! her angers wax
With waning of my youthful ways,
Daily wilt,[332] Ale! daily dwindle,
Swindle[333] me of salad-days.[334]

80

God of Death in Saki's guise[335]
Shall come to serve his blacken'd ale,
On drinking it the tipsy man's
Consciousness for good shall fail,
That Final Loss of Consciousness,
That Final Saki, Final Urn—
It shall be; so drink with care,
O Tipsy Tramp your Nectar-Churn.

81

As ye pour from fleshly jug
O Maiden mine, pulsating[336] wine,
As goblet-gall is brought at last
By the Final Saki's queued up brine,
My palms forget the goblet-touch,
And tongue forgets the wine-taste,
Do whisper then ye in my ears
Of Nectar, Pegs and Tavern-zest.[337]

82

As Death-duty, place on my lips
A Goblet, and no Basil leaf,
No Ganges-drop should grace my tongue,
Drip Malt-wine o' the brightest sheaf,[338]
O carriers of my corpse a-numb,
Corse-walkers[339] who cremate me,—
Chant not, "True be Lord, thy Name,"
Say— "Hail, O Tavern's symmetry!"

83

Do let those cry on my corpse
Whose wine-tears are shed for me,
My corpse set nigh, let them supply
Ale-fragrant sigh, in drunken spree;
The carriers of my body must
Shoulders lend with tipsy toes,
Light my pyre[340] where has been
Some Drinkers'-Nook, whose story goes.

84

Pour no myrrh[341] but, on my pyre,
Pure wine with goblets pour,
With Grape-tendril my death-urn wreath
But waterless— pour wine galore,
In memorium,[342] to revere[343] me
Darling, you must do something,—
Briskly ope' the tavern key,
All drunkards to the tavern bring.

85

If someone asks the corpse's name,
Dub me just " 'A Drunkard True,'
One that poured and made all pour
Liqueurs of the finest brew,"
If someone asks my caste or breed,
Tell him "Bedlam fair," and "he
Belonged to the goblet creed
And told at the Tavern's rosary."[344]

86

Tiding—![345] "Death-God approaching
With his deathly, darkened ale!"
Made Pundits forget manuscripts,
The Sage forgot his beads and bell,
The Priest forgot to worship and
The Wise forgot their wisdom all,
Yet, in death, none doth forget
A Drinker True, his Drinking Hall.

87

If God o' Death takes me, in faith,
Let me walk with liqueur fine,
Let 'em walk too— the barmaids coy—
Carrying hence[346] all goblets mine;
To Heaven's maze[347] or a sundry place
Or Hell, where you wish, take me,
If I can bond with Tavern Grace
Every place will equal be.

88

If drinking is a sinning act,
Then sins abound in Tavern's Three,
They too sin— my Goblet and
The Saki and that Wine-tree;
Hence, to mete out[348] justice, I
Must take them all to hell with me,
Wherever I am imprisoned,
May imprisoned the Tavern be.

89

Volcanic fires of which heart
Did wine temper,[349] Saki true?
Yet, "Gimme[350] more that wine galore—"
Strut drunkards all of bedlam-brew;
Every 'goer', passing soul,
Here varied wishes leave behind,
Turn wishful cravings to engravings,[351]
Pub becomes their grave unkind.

90

The Liqueur which I thirsted for—
That trance-potion—[352] I did not get;
I hankered for my prized Goblet,
But that denied, I took to fret;[353]
The Barmaid who I sauntered[354] for
Madly, She did Love me Not;
The Pub for which I madly craved,
I did not get (I'm denial-wrought!).[355]

91

The ken, too nigh! Do visions lie?
Gem-like beaded Hippocrene
Near at hand—yet far away—
The Goblets in their golden sheen;
I said "Enow,[356] I'll get them now!"
Though e'er receding,[357] pursued[358] them;
They deprive[359] (the more I crave) ;
Horizon—![360] My Tavern's frame!

92

Darkness of Despair surrounds
At times, hides the nectar peg,
Wine-radiance in secret bounds,
Hides the barmaid, with her keg;
Hope, at times, illumines[361]
My goblet with a sparkle 'gain,[362]
A game of hide-and-seek too fine
My Tavern plays, to state it plain.[363]

93

"Come forward, come" says Saki but
She retracts[364] her beckoning palm,
She urges me, "Sip your goblet,"
Displaces it with teaseful[365] charm;
Hardly do I know through what
Swerving miles 'twill drag me hence,
I forward move, it e'er recedes—
Tavern retracts in connivance.[366]

94

Woe! Slips the graceful goblet when
'Tis just about to reach my palm,
Just before they reach my lips
Liquors spill like wasteful psalm,[367]
O willful Walkers[368] of the World,
Come, marvel[369] on my wondrous luck,
My Tavern, I by degrees miss—
'Tis Going— Going— Gone; Alack!

95

If My Share of Wine is not
Lotted, let it be extinct,
If I get not, may extinct be
All goblets from the earth's precinct;[370]
'Tis not too far, that I should quit,
Nor close enough that I may drink,
My zest— in vain— a Mirage again,
Elusive,[371] that tavern-kink.

96

Ale Delays and Ale Denies,
What's the point in Tempting then?
No ale, nor peg I get, and yet,
Ah! Cruel Cup, ye tempt again?
What's lotted can't be blotted,
On my forehead Fate hath writ—[372]
"Thy Nectar-rill[373] shall distant flow
But close to heart thy Tavern's knit."

97

Long have I sat in this pub
With not a drop of ale to drink,
Careful, Rapt,[374] I fill my peg,
(Which) Someone topples, spills the brink;
In school I learnt— "Than Destiny,
Human zeal is stronger much,"
Yet, "Man is weak, and Fate is all—'"
The Tavern preaches sermons such.

98

For a Grail I searched, but woe, alas!
Destiny granted an 'empty bin,'
For doe-eyed lass I searched, but I
Was destined to deerskin;
Did any man ill-comprehend[375]
His fate, in manners that deceived?
On searching for my Tavern, I,
Urns of Death, from Fate received.

99

I do Love that goblet which
Beckons me from a distant palm,
I Love the wine which is the wine
From a distant face and lip lukewarm;[376]
No Love there is in Love begot,
True Love, in Love's yearning is,
Had I got my Nectar-Nook
It would not seem so sweet a bliss.

100

Meagre though, the barmaid keeps
Opulence[377] in Pleasure-Ale,
Which this world doth yearn to drink;
Come, come and take thy Fatal Grail!
Railing, shoving[378] some proceed
Though most are buried underneath,
Life's battle it is not, but
A thronging throe, that Tavern-Heath.

101

Meagre 'tis your liquor stock,
O my Barmaid, why must you
Eager Seekers bedlams turn,
With promise of that tipsy brew?
As we're ground[379] in daily death,
You abound in secret mirth,
Of our pain, make games again,
Aye Pub, Alas! You mock this earth.

102

O Saki, if a struggling man
Shoves forward his Life's Glass,
He gets to drink not more than two
Drops of your Fine Ale, alas!
A lifelong toil — eternal broil —[380]
Is looted by just drops a-pair,
To swindle simple human folk
The Tavern is the Cause unfair.

103

One that keeps me thirsty thus,
May that Wine Eternal be,
Eternal be the Peg that drives
Me to run thus, ceaselessly;[381]
No Tipsy Tongue doth ever curse
Anyone, nor bring to book,
Though you keep me sorrow-cloy'd,[382]
May Gaiety grasp you, Nectar-Nook!

104

Wish I not to forward move
To snatch another's cup-full ale,
Wish I not to others shove
And snatch their pegs by brawny[383] flail;
At me, O Barmaid, look ye not,
Lust I not as a craving crook,
No little joy it is, that I,
With eyes behold the Nectar-Nook!

105
Wine, Madeira, Nectar, Ale—
If names may turn me tipsy-toes,
With wine pegs below my lips
What might come of me, who knows?
Barmaid, close up not to me,
I may go mad if senses fail,
My thirsting self is hearty; I
Greet and grant you Nectar-Dale!

106
Is it for me so important,
That I should be a mendicant,
And ask the barmaid to grant me
Goblets with intoxicant?
If boozing begets heartiness,
There's no true love for Winsome Drop,
As for me, I turn Bedlam
Just on hearing- 'Nectar-Thorpe!'[384]

107

Though themselves were mendicants,
They promised me things important,
They could not give when I did crave,
Nor Goblet, nor Intoxicant;
Considerate of mortal weakness,
Nothing, e'er, to them I say,
But when the Tavern sees me now,
Abashed, She turns the other way!

108

There was a time of contentment
When I was gay with meagre ale,
Simple was my serving lass
And little was my nectar-grail,
This Heaven of my Little World,
At ease, the earthly evils took,
On a global sprawl[385] 'tis lost in all—
My teeny-weeny[386] Nectar-Nook!

109

Myriad Madeira-marts beheld,
Ample liqueurs, ale, I saw,
Varied grails and goblets held
In my palms, felt nectars raw,
One by one the barmaids served,
Each prettier than the rest,
None did to my eyes appeal,
None like Archaic[387] Tavern's 'Best!'

110

Once upon my lips would ply
Lapping wine: Ah, winsome past!
From my arms swung tipsy pegs,
"Once Upon A Time" is hears'd;[388]
The past saw me in embraces
Of wanton Sakis, hob-nob-clan;[389]
Desolate,—[390] now Urn of Death,
That was a Pub, O drinking man!

111
Lit furnace of a burning heart,
Drew wine of my tearfulness;
My moments trim,[391] they overbrim
My chalice-eyen,[392] in-medias-res;[393]
Eyes today are barmaids; cheeks
Drink from 'em and pinkish turn;
Dub me not ye melancholic,
I'm a walking-talking Wine-Barn.[394]

112
It changes hue, and oh! How quick!
My fickle, frisky wine, alas!
How quick in fistful friction it
Erodes away— My Wine Glass!
So quickly dwindles attraction
Of barmaids ('em, I o'erlook),
The morning showed the diff'rence; Aye!
Nightly Swindler— Nectar-Nook!

113
With every drop of ale belied[395]
Wine will keep you thirsting so,
From your palm, that temper-peg,
Circumstance may snatch and go;
O drinking lot, don't ever ride
On sweet trillings of barmaids hence;
There was a day when taverns would
Praise me beyond temperance!

114
All '–isms,'[396] paths and opinions
I quit, to be dubbed— 'Tipsy-True',
Wine wished to wash my feet
When pegs I broke in rendezvous;[397]
Now, that once-proud Nectar-Nook
Dogs me like a stalker;[398] why?
The reason? Well, I forsook[399] it,
And this the tavern knows, say I.

115
Think ye not I drank arrack
When I got no ale refined,
Nor drank I from the voodoo-skull[400]
When I could choose the goblet kind;
Unkindly, I did singe my heart
Which was by then burnt, and lo—
I chose Death-Urn, well, my Tavern
Implored[401] me to come back, though!

116
Free-flowing ale—— they came and went,
Quenched this Tavern's thirsting throe,
E'ermore, the grails galore
Broke, and did in pieces go,
Umpteen[402] barmaids rounded up[403]
Their daily jobs and farther went,
Umpteen drinkers came to drink—
Unchanged remains but Tipsy-Tent!

117

Remembering all luscious lips
Is possible not, by Wine frail;
And, are all the seeking hands
Remembered by Crazy Grail?
How many Drinkers' faces may
An Innocent Saki then recall?
Unique stands the Tavern lone,
Amidst the wanton[404] drinkers all!

118

Door to door I called and craved
"O Wine Grail!" "O Tipsy pub!"
I got no Tipsy Tavern, True,
For sooth, I got no drinking cup;
Then we met, but pleasures of
Meeting were not lotted, so,
Now that I've settled down,
My Love-Tavern tramps evermore.

119

I AM in the NECTAR-NOOK,
In my hands— the nectar cup,
The tavern's in this chalice, now
In reflection, shall all show up;
This weaving and unweaving hath
All my life, at leisure, took—
In me rests the Tavern or
I AM in the NECTAR-NOOK!

120

Who relates not to his Drink?
Who elates[405] not with his Glass?
Varied wines of umpteen kinds
Are in this Tavern's Universe!
At our will we glasses fill,
At our will we tipsy be,
Selfsame Saki serves us all,
Selfsame is the Tavern-key.

121
Volcanic Fires of my Heart
Winsome Wine can temper, true,
This goblet-sect can well reflect
All my life's moments too;
Tavern True 'tis not where just
Ale is 'sold!' (Ah, baleful 'trade'!)
The one that gives me tipsy toes
Is Nectar-Nook, my Happy Glade!

122
That tipsiness from wine I drew,
Then divorced the drink itself,
Met madness in that goblet-brew;
Gave up the cup! (I could not help!)
Met Saki after Saki but
Togetherness I could not brace,
Drank sweetness fro' the Nook and I
Then forgot its very face!

123

It knocks now at th' tavern gate,
That clumsy, hollow, fatal cup;
Cold and deep sighs exhale
All the drinkers at the pub;
How scant youth's elixir was,
Woe! How little I could taste!
Too quick closed the gates of my
Life's Nectar-Nook: Ah, waste!

124

Whither hath Godly Sakis fled?
Whither hath Fragrant Wines gone?
Whither, the Dreamland-Tavern, is?
Whither, the Golden-Cup, lovelorn?
The drinking lot did value not
Their claret-velvet-wine then,
Now left with pubs and goblets none,
They look for their Old Pub again!

125

'Unique' hold the drinkers all,
Liqueurs served in their heydays,[406]
'Magic' was their miracle-cup
In era of their youthful ways,
Yet, if you ask grey-haired clans,
You shall get the answer same—
"Not one is left of Drinkers Great,
No Tavern True is there to name!"

126

Lowly 'Booze' I cleansed in faith,
'Pure' my ale is 'Wine' today,
The minion 'Meena'—407 'Honey-pot',
Let 'Chalice' be the bluish 'Bay';
No wonder Muezzins, Pundits shriek,
"Audacious!" they dub my take,
My 'Courtesan and Wine-song',
Of my 'Tavern' I do make!

127
Of heartstrings and deep intents,
A clean breast the wine makes;
Untold tales and secrets deep,
Oft and on the goblet rakes;
Barely by her gestures, signs,
Meanings all, the Saki sees;
Yet, till date, for those who drink,
An Enigma,[408] the Tavern is!

128
The more intense the depth of hearts,
The deeper is the goblet grace;
Stronger the intoxicant,
Stronger the mind's tipsiness;
Philosophy…the more you have,
The prettier shall your Saki be;
The juicier your humours are,
Juicy Tavern serves in glee.

129

Happy, luscious lips they are,
Who touch a wee-bit of my wine,
Crazy turn the cozy clutches
Which hold up that goblet mine,
Eyes pop out, O Onlooker,
If you, at my Saki, stare,
Those who enter Tavern mine
Turn Bedlam, by Nectar's snare.

130

On ev'ry tongue shall roll, now on,
My very pure Wine, in sooth;
Every clutch shall flaunt the Cup
Which my Saki serves with truth;
Houses all shall murmur of
My Wine-Seller's fine trade,
Courtyards all will turn into
My Frankincensed[409] Nectar-Glade.

131

In my wine did one and all
Find their own wines too,
In my drinking cup they found
Their own drinking goblets true,
In my pretty barmaid they
Saw their pretty Sakis all;
Tastes of men, they varied then
In beholding the Drinking Hall!

132

Tears of the Nectar-Nook— 'tis
Not wine, as you plainly think;
Eyes of the Tavern— those
Goblets, whence you daily drink;
Fine memories of the past,
Dance as barmaids, gaily brook;
No courtyard of a poet's heart,
That Maze, Melancholy— Nectar-Nook!

133
Cravings to Despair to Trash
Turned all, in brewing the ale,
Yearnings turned into mere ash
In the making of the grail!
Drinkers, after drinking, will
Move on; and no one will know
How myriad towering wishes burnt
In Tavern craft, its waxing glow.

134
O Universe! If my Ale is able
To displace the Gall of life,
If my Saki serves you well
(you may trust that foster-wife!),
If your hollow watches now,
My tavern-echo resounding take,
The birth of 'Nectar-Nook' will be
Worth the Dawn to which Birds Wake.

135
Reared I have, with reverence great,
Voluptuous wine and Saki Girl,
Who lifted goblets full of wine
That only in did thoughts unfurl;
With love and respect stirred too well,
Treat Saki and this Tavern-Book,
Here, O World! I Give You All!
I give my heart-borne Nectar-Nook!

End Notes

1. Dignified, reverently held (esp. for drinking).
2. She/He who pours/serves intoxicating and satiating drinks; barmaid / bar-man / one who serves wine.
3. 'Cup' and 'dance' used as a verb and a noun respectively; a deliberate inversion for poesy's sake.
4. The Tavern's liquid charms.
5. Hippocrene is synonymous with a Romantic, transformative drink (c.f. Keats' 'Ode to a Nightingale'); mythically, an eternally-flowing fountain that churns out transformative ale/liquid.
6. Coalesce or superimpose; two-in-one.
7. Religious rites.
8. Shelter(ed) from the (rough) winds; undisturbed.
9. Horde; group; flock.
10. Dry; also suggestive of the idiomatic idea of those 'high and dry'.
11. Thoughts
12. Unreal and imaginary (may also mean unearthly and ghostly in certain circumstances).
13. Simplicity; in a simpleton's manner or in a fool's demeanour.
14. (Predicament of being) Of two minds; indecision.
15. Leading to silence; leading to stasis or standstill.
16. Walk.
17. Expression of sorrow or regret.
18. Road or path.
19. Holds motionless.
20. The one at a distance; that; over there.
21. Repeat; keep on saying.
22. Liquor; ale.
23. Claret- Red (dark-purplish) like Bordeaux Wine; Ale- Beer-like drink made of rapidly fermented malts and hops.

24. The tavern or pub; the drink arena.
25. Wine or ale in this context.
26. Listen; pay heed to.
27. Noise; clamour.
28. Soiree- A fashionable session (of tingling music etc., a musical, in a party); A fashionable session of tingling music in this context, to give it the effect of and nearness to the Indian instrument 'Jaltarang'.
29. Noise produced by stringed instrument (by moving fingers across strings to play it).
30. Kissing.
31. A humourous rhyming poem (of five lines with a rhyme scheme of aabba).
32. Limbeck- Alembic, or distilling apparatus, for wine / spirits etc. (Shakespearean word) The limbeck-bearer is the Saki in this context.
33. One with an attractive / decorative surface; whatever aims at transforming something / someone (Here liquour transforms the drinker); one that has the objective of producing something new from something old.
34. A long-handed tool, stouter at the end, for beating grain (used for producing malt-wine too).
35. Henna- Organic, decorative dye used on bridal palms; Ornate- Decorated.
36. Synesthetically superimposed- The cup is beaded with gems and filled with nectar-like wine; vision and taste entwine.
37. Crepe- Silk / Cotton cloth wrinkled for finesse (acting as veil in this context)
38. Geisha- An Oriental girl (usu. Japanese) trained to entertain men by singing, dancing and serving (wine etc.); Golden-Geisha – Saki.
39. The drinking glass (in this context), not related to the Christian Theological Literature pertaining to the Holy Grail.
40. A variant of deep Blue, akin to the Teal-Duck's wings.
41. Ring out; make series of sounds; be clamourous.

42. A meeting of lovers (the drinkers and their Nectar-Nook in this context) at a secret time / place (to win over the soulmate); a clandestine meeting to achieve something.

43. The spirit or zeal contained in the colourful spectrum of the rainbow, the spirit which is reflected in the entire universe.

44. Show of unwillingness or seeming dissatisfaction or being disagreeable.

45. Soothe or make more agreeable by action (but here the action is one of temporary abstinence or denial- 'temperance'- at first, which makes drinking all the more agreeable, since everything is not given away in one go, but in installments).

46. Showing abstinence in actions (of drinking, flirting, gorging etc.); practice of drinking little alcohol; moderation in indulgence (of appetites).

47. Fearless.

48. Sexually playful.

49. Carefully formed / manufactured and embellished.

50. Obtained

51. Foaming and splashing (of liquid, ocean etc.)

52. A stream-like flow; liquid in flux.

53. Cleansed through sifters and sieves.

54. Of sorrow; Pang- Sorrow.

55. Able to bend without breaking.

56. Barrel-like container for liquids (wine etc.)

57. Time and again; over and over again; repeatedly.

58. Earthly.

59. Glass container.

60. Plural of 'Poesy' / Poetry; a body of poems.

61. Severely hurt.

62. Frighten.

63. Delve deep; go deep within; enter with force; make a sharp entry into.

64. Burn.

65. Drinking (Sl.).

66. Madhouse; People belonging to lunatic asylum / Bedlam.

67. Esteemed people (Pundits, Momins, Clergies) in the religious orders of Hindus, Muslims and Christians

respectively.

68. Net (which makes one captive).

69. Teething through- Biting and ripping to make one's way out.

70. A term borrowed from the theorist Jacques Lacan (and Helene Cixous), in a pseudo-theoretical manner, to etch the Nectar-Nook's vinous juices as well as the multiplicative, ever-increasing aura of the intoxicants and its phallic 'pleasure principle' (c.f. Lacan); also the feminine physical-spiritual sexual rapture (c.f. Cixous) found therein.

71. Something immense; Great (derived from the name of the huge elephant, now extinct).

72. You; colloquial and plural pronoun for the second person 'you'.

73. Short periods of time during which something is done or some act is undertaken.

74. Sacrilege; act of irreverence; negation of / avoiding a sacrament.

75. Lacking in humour (wittiness) and 'humours' i.e. fluids in human body determining a person's temperament.

76. Group; members of a group taken together.

77. Holy river for the Hindus, flowing from the Northern Himalayas to Eastern India.

78. Exactly the same.

79. Strings of beads used by the Roman Catholics for counting prayers (similar stringed beads for counting prayers are used by the Hindus and Muslms too).

80. In great amount.

81. Melodic uttering of prayer.

82. Lord Shiva, or Kaal-Bhairav, in oriental mythology, drinks wine and dopes by using cannabis, opium etc; also an equivocation, in that, Hindu philosophy preaches how Lord Shiva dopes with 'Siddhi' meaning cannabis as well as eternal or ideal Knowledge. (A bit similar to Dionysus, God of the grape-harvest, winemaking and ritual madness in occidental mythology).

83. Ring, peal

84. A person appointed to recite prayers in a mosque.

85. Acclamation / greeting wishing one good.

86. A bit open.

87. Lacking company; having no one beside; alone; desolate

88. Producing a (series of) quavering sound(s) or beats.

89. Cheerful variation in song, tune etc.

90. Lady Luck is Fickle Fortune, akin to the Goddess Lakshmi in oriental mythology; 'Chance' personified as a controlling power in human affairs.

91. Rakes up the nightly fire (to keep awake); also, collects, gathers, draws together (viz. drinkers and their experiences in this context).

92. Yes; Aye- derived from the utterances in British Parliament during voting, suggesting 'yes'. (Ayes- Yes; Noes-No)

93. Blackness of Death also alludes to the complexion of the Death-God 'Yama' in Indian Mythology.

94. Weaken; fail; decay; fall.

95. Victorious; one that wins over others.

96. Honestly, truly etc., archaic use 'in faith'.

97. Worthless; failing to keep up standards.

98. Uninhabited; lonely.

99. Large celebrations / parties.

100. Keep vigil; guard.

101. Picturesque- Good to view, beautiful; She- Pronoun used as a noun, for 'Saki' or limbeck-bearer.

102. Unique; matchless.

103. Travel (travel together, in this context).

104. Unbalanced; asymmetrical.

105. As a couple / duo; together.

106. Sorrowful, gloomy.

107. Quota; allowance.

108. Maniacs who abstain from drinking alcohol totally.

109. Biting; grinding with incisors (while uttering things filthy).

110. Foul; abominable.

111. Drinking (Sl.).

112. Bitter complaint; vehement denunciation.

113. Help time pass pleasantly.

114. Indicative of death

115. A sorrowful celebrations among Muslims, commemorating Prophet Muhammad's grandson Hussain's death.
116. An event which, as if, threatens, forebodes something disastrous.
117. Though sorrowful for the demonic clans, the burning of Holika's pyre is a happy Hindu festival, a celebration for those who champion good over evil.
118. Holika was a demoness in Hindu mythology, who was burnt to death with help of God Vishnu. The story of *Holika dahan* (Holika's death by burning, in order to save Prahlad) signifies the triumph of good over evil.
119. Upward gushing wave / tide (of fire, in this context).
120. Made to come (from).
121. Gloomy.
122. Glamourous.
123. A Muslim happy-feast marking the end of the fast of *Ramadan* and the sacrifice of Abraham / Ibrahim.
124. Happy.
125. A day of shows, to embellish and look good.
126. Weaves; is woven of; is created on a large-scale like never-ending networks in fabrics (the noun 'looms' is used as a verb)
127. A Hindu spring-festival of natural colours, honouring Lord Krishna (similar to the Spanish 'La Tomatina' festival).
128. Producing a euphoric sigh (of relief, satisfaction etc.)
129. Bets a-flung; Wagered.
130. Hindu festival of lights commemorating Lord Rama's return to Ayodhya after defeating Ravana; signifies the victory of good over evil.
131. One who nurtures, nurses, brings up.
132. One who bears (in womb).
133. The mother who suckles her child (Mother as the first Saki for all humans)
134. The nourishing liquid / the drink required for rearing children; milk.
135. Blessing.
136. Medicine; healing drug.

137. Clay.
138. Associated with wine.
139. Drinking greedily.
140. Unquenched; never satisfied.
141. Onrush; raid (to obtain something).
142. 'In troth' is archaic, meaning 'truly'.
143. Drunkards.
144. Signs (in nature etc.) foreboding something.
145. Occur; take place; happen.
146. Please.
147. Sun
148. Hearty; of health.
149. River Indus / *Sindhu*, in the Western part of India.
150. Happen to return again and again; take place repeatedly.
151. Delve deep; go deep within; enter with force; make a sharp entry into.
152. In continuous strain, like a never-ending reel of thread.
153. Makes (them) wet.
154. Satiates.
155. Decorated with / strewn with stars.
156. Breeze.
157. Upon.
158. Drown.
159. All; of every type; common.
160. Move about; rove.
161. An item.
162. Vision.
163. Perhaps.
164. Desire.
165. Mixes.
166. Archaic for beggar'd or beggary; practicing beggary (also 'mendicancy').
167. Pertaining to bees.
168. Cluster / group.
169. Small patch of greenery or clearing; light forest.
170. Open.
171. Spill out.
172. Perfume-house; perfumes collectively; C.f. the sense of 'All Arabia breathes...' in 'Rape of the Lock' by

Alexander Pope.

173. An example of 'Synesthesia'— perfumes 'tasted' by cuckoo birds!
174. The call of cuckoos.
175. Act of producing fruits.
176. Drinking vessels having stems and bases.
177. Soothing; calming.
178. Having a pleasant odour.
179. Pours in; gradually introduces.
180. Of a state of numbness or suspended sensibility.
181. New-born.
182. Lustre.
183. Shaded, leafy recesses; a country retreat.
184. Ecstatic; of spiritual joy.
185. To draw or pull.
186. Girl; young woman (Australian Sl.).
187. A coarse, nubby fabric.
188. Decorate
189. Numerous.
190. Lose oneself- Turn mad.
191. 'Tis- poetical use meaning 'it is'.
192. A disorderly retreat (from drunkenness), much like a hangover.
193. Satisfying (thirst or hunger).
194. Decreasing.
195. Whether desired or not.
196. Abnormality; irregularity (in life etc.).
197. Sleepy-eyed or sleeping.
198. Bounty- Reward (the barmaid herself is a reward, due to her youthful graces).
199. Increasing.
200. Serf or slave; the drinker is a serf here; since he / she, though winsome, is enslaved by the Saki and the drink.
201. Pertaining to dosage (medicinal jargon).
202. Wander about (in moving, shifting vision).
203. Not constant.
204. Constant.
205. Deviate; wander.
206. Exhibits ostentatiously.

207. Spilling.

208. Cover with sweet fragrance, in this context.

209. Displaying wooing behaviour to get favours.

210. Lord Krishna; he performed *Tapaswa, Yoga*; he meditated and observed celibacy for twelve years even though he had his wife Rukmini (who too meditated with him), only to purge himself of the evils of libido before planning a child. As he gained total control over his mind by dint of Yoga, he is called the King of Yoga or *Yogiraj*.

211. Tones of definite pitch.

212. Sonatina- A short sonata; brief composition of about four independent movements, varying in key, mood and tempo. (The Saki has such attribute).

213. Utmost; to the greatest limit; completely.

214. Minor, major, sharp are all musical terms.

215. A glass of drink raised in one's honour / health.

216. Resounds; Echoes.

217. A sudden indulgence.

218. A plate marking time (in hours) and a gnomon casting shadows to calculate it.

219. Colours.

220. Detach from something to which they are strongly adhered. (E.g. the juice from the pulp).

221. Removing or drawing something out; cutting.

222. 'Flower' has been used as a verb.

223. A male duck.

224. Hankers; yearns; moans (for).

225. 'Mansarovar' is, literally, 'a lake created in the mind' or 'mind-wrought lake'. Hindu mythology states that a lake (the Holy Mansarovar, now in China occupied Tibet) was created in the mind of Lord Brahma before being manifested on earth. The Nectar-Nook is being equated to it.

226. Them.

227. Reference to the Hindu Goddess Kali, the bearer of 'Kaal' or time, who, at the same time, is benevolent as well as malevolent.

228. Where sacrifices are made.

229. Once again.
230. One who denies the existence of God.
231. Place of refuge.
232. Permission to enter.
233. Aimless wanderer.
234. Manner of walking.
235. Without belief for religion (here the tavern is the drinker's religion).
236. Adhered to.
237. Group.
238. Used as 'loaded' (with goodies, materialistic stuff) as is loaded on ship's deck, and/or 'decorated' with things pertaining to the pleasure principles of humankind.
239. To 'doll up' is to decorate oneself with embellishments and toiletry.
240. Well-dressed.
241. Sheikh / Sheik is a Muslim (usu. Arab) religious official, (also) a romantically alluring man (Sl.).
242. Favourite.
243. Allah- Muslim name for God; The Supreme Being.
244. Yore- Time past.
245. Synchronization; harmony.
246. Hostility.
247. Unite; blend.
248. A Muslim who offers Namaaz / prayers.
249. A Hindu Brahmin, learned and versatile in Hindu Scriptures.
250. Wine.
251. Willingly; gladly.
252. Abstain.
253. One that calls.
254. Estimation.
255. To be honest.
256. Form group.
257. Proud; indignant.
258. The
259. Uncovers; shows up.
260. Proscribed by society as improper.
261. The next day; tomorrow.

262. Kink- Twist.

263. Seer.

264. Mahomet- (Anglicised word for) Mohammed, the Prophet.

265. Gleaming faintly.

266. Purify; extract some components.

267. Inebriated; drunk.

268. Vedic ritualistic drink with energizing qualities.

269. Chirp; youthful, trendy conversations.

270. Dronacharya, the teacher with elite wisdom in Hindu mytholgy.

271. Discard; avoid.

272. Mythological (Hindu) Sea / Ocean;
Varuni or Varunani is the female consort of God Varuna; the goddess was adopted by Varuna when she came out of the ocean, during the churning for *amrita* (immortal nectar). She represents the
purifying nectar of immortality and is the agent of transcendental wisdom.

273. Heavenly.

274. Rambha- An enchanting *Apsara* (female spirit of clouds and oceans) in Hindu mythology.

275. Temperament; disposition.

276. To hold ground; (also) to stand; to bear (and oppose).

277. Polluted.

278. Feel intoxicated (Sl).

279. A hundred (100); perhaps derived from the unit of internal capacity (100 cubic feet) of ships, related to immersion and buoyancy.

280. Singlehandedly; alone.

281. Exhausting labour.

282. Charitable distribution.

283. Unsuccessful.

284. Ken- Gaze; vision; cognizance.

285. Foolish; illiterate.

286. C.f. Socialism and equality, born of the revolutionary cries of 'Liberty, Equality, Fraternity'.

287. Pub-born- born in the pub; containing pub philosophy; akin to the ideals of the 'inn-club' intelligentsia, revolutionary in a way, bringing *inqilaab* or revolution to a nation.

288. Inexperienced in drinking, in this context.

289. Release from grasp.

290. Favours granted by someone superior or divine.

291. Give life to it; make sprightly.

292. Glittering.

293. Arousing desire; highly pleasing to senses.

294. Sheds drops.

295. Face.

296. Double.

297. Tapestry- Decoration; adorned form.

298. Specialized skill (sense nearly obsolete now).

299. Devoid of feelings.

300. Artfully shy; coquettish.

301. Li'l measure- Little or small amount; short lease.

302. Goodbye.

303. Nigh- Near. Life as placed in close proximity with Death.

304. Non-stop; without pause.

305. Constantly; in a steadfast manner.

306. Belle- Lass; girl.

307. Fears of losing.

308. The state of being cheerful.

309. Too little.

310. Trap.

311. Sharpens.

312. Allotted share.

313. A sudden burst of ill-temper.

314. Spirituous liquour of low quality (e.g. Toddy).

315. Bestow excessive love.

316. Fanciful and whimsical (arch.)

317. Kick.

318. Truth; in truth, truly (archaic).

319. Having little tensile strength.

320. Earthly and destroyable.

321. Small.

322. Rejuvenating drink; magic potion.

323. Things left at the bottom of a vessel / cup.

324. Beat up.

325. Involves.

326. Sustain; be subject to.

327. Speak in spitefully critical manner.

328. Consolation.

329. Oblivion.

330. Sick.

331. Bane- Curse.

332. Wither.

333. Fraudulently deceive.

334. A Shakespearean idiomatic expression; refers to heydays, when a person is youthful and at his prime. (C.f Shakespeare's *Antony and Cleopatra*)

335. Disguise.

336. Throbbing; exciting.

337. Enthusiasm.

338. A bundle of reaped grain.

339. Corse- (same as) Corpse; corse-walkers- those who accompany the corpse to burial or cremation.

340. Structure of wood for burning a corpse.

341. Aromatic resin, like oil, derived from a plant.

342. Memory.

343. Regard, with respect.

344. Tavern's rosary… made of wine goblets, as stated earlier in the poem.

345. News.
346. From here.
347. Confusing network of paths.
348. Mete out- Administer.
349. Turn sober.
350. Give me (colloq.).
351. Writings / designs made by cutting / chipping / corroding hard surfaces (as on graves in this context).
352. Medicine that leads to a semi-conscious state.
353. Brood; brooding.
354. Leisurely rambled.
355. Denial-wrought- Accustomed to receiving a 'no' for an answer.
356. Enough.
357. Retreating; withdrawing.
358. Chased.
359. Disallow enjoyment (of something).
360. The ever receding and intangible line where the sky meets the earth.
361. Fills with light.
362. Again.
363. State it plain- State it in a simple manner.
364. Takes / moves back.
365. In a bid to tease.
366. Assents to wrong-doing (by the Saki, in this context).
367. A sacred hymn.
368. Travellers; those who infest.
369. Feel the wonder; be astonished.
370. Space; limits; boundary.
371. Skillfully evasive; one that gives the slip.
372. Written.
373. Nectar-rill- Wine-brook; rill- rivulet.
374. Engrossed.

375. Ill-comprehend- Badly understand.

376. Tepid; moderately warm.

377. Richness.

378. Pushing.

379. Past Tense of 'grind'.

380. Broil- Annoyance.

381. Endlessly.

382. Cloy'd- Covered overabundantly.

383. Muscular.

384. Thorpe- Village.

385. Ungracefullyspread out.

386. Tiny.

387. Of earlier / ancient days.

388. Placed on a corpse carrying vehicle.

389. Group that drinks together (Arch.)

390. Lonely/ left alone.

391. Trim- Pruning/ clipping / reducing by cutting off.

392. Eyen- Eyes (Arch.)

393. 'In the Middle of Things'

394. Barn- Storing place; store-house.

395. Lied about (Arch.)

396. —isms – (opinions about) Theories, systems, orders etc.

397. A meeting between two people.

398. One who follows persistently.

399. Past Tense of 'forsake'. (Arch.)

400. A skull (from which wine can be drunk) related to the black-art, Voodoo.

401. Begged / prayed.

402. Too many (Sl.).

403. Rounded up- Completed / finished.

404. Lascivious.

405. Feels happy.

406. C.f. Salad days (stated earlier in the notes section)

407. A Saki / woman (in Arabic / Urdu), c.f. 'Meena
Bazaar' (a market for women); also a name of Parvati,
wife of Lord Shiva.
408. A puzzle or riddle.
409. Frankincense- Fragrant plant resin; Frankincensed-
embalmed with fragrant plant resin.

ABOUT THE AUTHOR

TUHIN SANYAL loves poetic strain. This love affair dates back to his school days which he prefers to call "the wonder years of cadence". His alma-maters being St. Mary's O & D School (Dum Dum, Calcutta) and St. Joseph's College (Bowbazar, Calcutta), Tuhin is presently an Assistant Professor in English at Tufanganj College in Cooch Behar, India. He is a published poet and has authored books like *White, Blue and Other Poems* (2004) and *Phoenix on a Female Body and Other Poems* (2009), both published by Writers Workshop, Calcutta. As a P.G. student at the University of Calcutta, he employed blank verse to pen a satirical collage-play titled *Measure-Unmeasure* — an onstage publication (and directorial debut) based on all the works of William Shakespeare — which has been archived in the *Millennium Link Project* of Shakespeare's Birthplace Trust at Stratford-upon-Avon, London, in the year 2000; and it has been recorded in the online History of the English Department of the University of Calcutta. In the year 2002, the University of Calcutta awarded him with an M.Phil. degree (in English) and applauded his thesis on *Yeats and the Dialectics of his Imagination*.

To earn his bread and ale, Tuhin began his career as a high-school English teacher at St. Xavier's School, Bokaro, where he taught for a couple of years before being appointed as an Assistant Teacher (P.G., English) at A.B. Vidyamandir, Athpur, by the West Bengal Regional School Service Commission. He has written for *The Times of India*, and has also been the Senior Sub-editor with *Echo of India*, two reputed Calcutta-based English dailies. He joined Tufanganj College, Cooch Behar, as an Assistant Professor in English, in 2010. Thereafter he has doubled up as Invited Lecturer at Salesian College, Sonada, Darjeeling (2011), at the nascent Cooch Behar Panchanan Barma University (2013-15) and at Netaji Subhas Open University (Cooch Behar centre). He says, "I am a part of all that I have met," much like Tennyson's Ulysses, and his varied experiences cry out "Hallelujah" with the spectrums of images, invectives and emotions encapsulated in his poetic expressions. Figuratively speaking, his poetic expressions give the effect of an inverted question mark—uncannily beautiful— starting from a dot or speck, and ending in a kink or hook, thus trapping the readers' attention in a curt and crisp manner. To him, "'Poetry' is the standard unit to measure human emotions, and the unit to state such measurement should therefore be the intuitive quotient, amount or intensity of 'Felt Poetry'."

Tuhin's first book *White, Blue and Other Poems* has been archived in The National Library of India with Call Number E 821 Sa 59 w. His poetic ventures have been mentioned in discussions by the poet and professor Dr. Rubana Ahmed (Bangladesh), by Prof. Sudha Rai (Rajasthan University) and by Prof Shyamala A. Narayan (Jamia Milia Islamia University). Poet Rubana Ahmed, in an edition of *The Daily Star* (Dec. 23, 2006, Vol.5 Num.915), even stated that of "good poetry after 1995," she "sense(s) fire in (the poems of) … Tuhin Sanyal." Tuhin has numerous well researched articles and published academic papers to his credit. His paper titled *Picassonian Cubism in the Eliotian Wasteland* earned him the prestigious B. T. Memorial Award, 2012, from Berhampur University (Odisha, India). Habitual rhyming and 'thinking aloud' by contributing to online spaces also etch his expressive strain, and he champions only "Felt Poetry" – his yardstick for good verses. Yet, more than 'Poetry', Tuhin loves 'Raina'— an embodiment of "pulsating, Felt Poetry"— his tiny daughter, who, according to him, "surpasses all art."

www.ingramcontent.com/pod-product-compliance
Lightning Source LLC
LaVergne TN
LVHW092020190726
843493LV00002B/518